WATCH OUT!

Dennis is back again, lassoing a laugh on every page of this latest volume of his saga of mischief.

Scallawag of the schoolroom, the nemesis of his neighbors, the plague (and pride) of his parents, America's favorite cartoon youngster celebrates his umpteenth book since he was "born" in 1951.

His fame (or notoriety) has spread across the United States and spilled over into 43 foreign countries by way of over 700 newspapers carrying his day-by-day misadventures.

Every week millions of television viewers chuckle at his antics on his own CBS show; his cocky little grin appears on products from pajamas to puppets; his comic book capers are young readers' favorites.

Let's face it—you can't escape him!

But one word of warning—when Dennis invades your living room, be on your guard—or he'll lasso your heart!

Other Books by Hank Ketcham in Fawcett Crest Editions:

TEACHERS THREAT

DENNIS THE MENACE...
TEACHER'S THREAT

By HANK KETCHAM

A Fawcett Crest Book

Fawcett Publications, Inc., Greenwich, Conn.
Member of American Book Publishers Council, Inc.

DENNIS THE MENACE . . . TEACHER'S THREAT was originally published
by Holt, Rinehart & Winston, Inc. This expanded edition,
prepared especially for Fawcett Publications, Inc., contains
62 additional cartoons which did not appear in the original, higher-
priced edition and is issued through arrangement with
Holt, Rinehart & Winston, Inc., and The Hall Syndicate, Inc.

● ● ● ● ● ● ● ●

Published by Fawcett World Library,
67 West 44th Street, New York, New York 10036.
Printed in the United States of America.

"HOW YA LIKE THAT *CRAZY PURPLE SHOE*?"

"RIGHT THERE ON MY CHEST. SEE? ISN'T THAT A HAIR?"

"YOU'RE NOT S'POSED TO READ WHEN YA HAVE COMPANY!"

"I'M JUST HAVIN' A FEW FRIENDS IN."

"LIKE I TOLD YA: WHEN YOU'RE IN A CROWD, *WATCH OUT FOR KNEES!*"

"SOME TEACHER! CAN SHE TEACH YA TO BLOW BUBBLE GUM? NAW!
CAN SHE TEACH YA TO SHOOT A SLINGSHOT? NAW! CAN SHE TEACH YA..."

"HI, MR. HARMON! DID YA EVER GET RID OF THOSE *TERMITES*?"

"WATER? I'M GETTIN' *DRY* CLEANED!"

"ALL YOU GOTTA DO IS FRY THE BACON AN' EGGS. I GOT THE *TOAST MADE!*"

"I WAS BORN IN OL' TRINIDAD! AN'
LEAVIN' THERE MAKES ME VERY SAD!
I WAS BORN IN OL'——

—— HEY, WHERE'S *TRINIDAD?*"

"IF DINNER'S READY, I'D BETTER GO OUT AND UNTIE DAD!"

"BOY, IF THAT WASN'T ME, I'D *LAUGH!*"

"YOU'RE OKAY, HAROLD. THAT WASN'T YOU. THE KID HERE JUST BROKE A WIENER ROASTING STICK!"

"WELL? DO YOUR BONES FEEL ANY STRONGER?"

"I DON'T *KNOW* WHAT HE DID! HE JUST KEEPS SAYING 'YOU'LL FIND OUT'!"

"HE WANTS TO SEE YOU ABOUT A POLICEMAN'S BALL... BUT _I_ DIDN'T TAKE IT!"

"IF YA DIDN'T WANT ME TO COME OVER SO MUCH, WHY'D YA BUY COLOR TV?"

"WE'RE SINGING HI DIDDLE-DIDDLE, DENNIS. SO WILL YOU KINDLY STOP YELLING 'GO!GO!GO!'?"

"KNOW WHY I'M UP SO EARLY, MR. WILSON?
ME 'N DAD ARE GOIN' *FISHIN'!*"

"I COULDN'T *FIND* A STOCKIN'!"

"I'M HIDIN' THESE SO SANTA CLAUS WON'T THINK I HAVE TOO MUCH ALREADY!"

"REMEMBER——THIS ISN'T JUST *ANY* OL' TREE!"

"HEY, *WAIT!* LET *ME* PAY FOR THAT!"

"SOMEBODY WANTED TO TALK TO DAD, BUT I HUNG UP 'CAUSE HE THOUGHT I WAS A *GIRL!*"

"I FINALLY MET THAT NEW KID ACROSS THE STREET."

"OKAY, THERE'S BUTTER ON MY HAND. *THAT* DON'T PROVE NOTHIN'!"

"MOM? IS PEOPLE'S TOOTHPASTE OKAY FOR DOGS?"

"BETTER LET *ME* EMPTY <u>THAT</u> POCKET!"

"HAVE ANOTHER COOKY, JOEY. I GOT *LOTS* MORE IN HERE!"

"HER NAME IS GINA. SHE'S BEEN LEARNIN' ME TO MAKE MUD PIZZAS"

"REMEMBER THAT LADY THAT WOULDN'T GIVE ME NONE OF HER POPCORN?"

"YOU COME RIGHT UP HERE AND GET IN THIS BED! THE DOCTOR IS WAITING!"

"WELL, THAT'S THE WAY THE COOKIES CRUMBLE..."

"WHY DO I HAVE TO DRESS UP TO COME HERE? WHO AM I TRYIN' TO *KID*?"

"*THIS* OUGHTA GIVE US ENOUGH ROOM IN THE POOL!"

"HOO WEE! IF YA THINK THAT'S BAD, SMELL *THIS* ONE!"

"KISS AN' HUG! KISS AN' HUG! SMACK YOUR SWEETIE ON THE MUG!...."

"IT'S THE ONE WITH THE STICKY DOOR HANDLES."

"MOM, WOULD YOU MIND TURNIN' THE TV ON?"

"**SOLD!** TO THE MAN HOLDING HIS HAND OVER HIS LITTLE BOY'S MOUTH!"

"MOM, HOW'D YOU LIKE TO FINISH MAKING SOME WAFFLES?"

"HOW COME MY PIGGY BANK DON'T RATTLE NO MORE?"

"'ANYBODY COULD FLUSH HIS SOCKS DOWN THE TOILET! NOBODY'S PERFECT!' THAT'S WHAT I SHOULDA SAID!"

"IS HE DEAD?"

"SEE? SEE HOW FLAT THEY ARE?"

"YOU'RE ALWAYS TALKIN' ABOUT THE 'GOOD OL' DAYS" WHEN I WASN'T HERE. WELL, *ENJOY* YOURSELVES!"

"JOEY'S MOM IS SICK, SO I'M TAKIN' HIM UNDER MY WING!"

"WILL YA STOP WORRYIN', JOEY? I'M NOT
GONNA SWIM OFF AN' *LEAVE* YA!"

"I'M GONNA TEACH RUFF HOW TO PLAY FETCH!"

"WHO'S MARGIE? AN' DOES MRS. WILSON KNOW
YOU'RE ALWAYS THINKIN' OF HER?"

"DOES NEW WALLPAPER COST VERY MUCH?"

"STEAK? AW, I THOUGHT WE WERE GONNA HAVE *HOTDOGS!*"

"DADDY SAID *THAT*?!"

"HEY, MOM! YOU'D BETTER FIX *PLENTY* OF DINNER!"

"GLAD TO MEET YOU WHERE'S YOUR BATHROOM?"

"I WANNA SEE HER TALK THE LEG OFF A CHAIR!"

"JUST WIGGLE YOUR FOOT QUIETLY. IT ISN'T NECESSARY
TO KEEP SAYING 'WAKE UP'!"

"Boy! Are you people ever missin' a good movie on telebision!"

"YOU MISSED A WRINKLE."

"CAN I USE HIM NEXT?"

"I'M GOIN' OVER TO THE WILSONS. I GOTTA GET SOME SLEEP!"

"WINDOWS ARE HANDY THINGS FOR CLEANIN' UP A ROOM!"

"DID YA EVER KNOCK 'EM **ALL** DOWN?"

"THAT'S WHAT I LIKE ABOUT SPEAR-FISHIN'.
AT LEAST YA *SEE* SOME FISH!"

"DON'T GET UP! I'LL JUST PULL UP A CHAIR!"

"JUST REMEMBER ... LITTLE KIDS *NEED* MASHED POTATOES!"

"'BOUT A MILLION KEEN LITTLE CARS TO RIDE IN, AN' I HAVE TO BE WITH SOMEBODY THAT LIKES TO *WALK!*"

"WE *FROWN* ON THAT AROUND HERE."

"GEE WHIZ, MOM! CAN'T YA LEAVE MY ROOM *NATURAL*?"

"NOT A BAD PARTY. I BUSTED SIX BALLOONS AN' A WINDOW!"

"WE'LL CALL THIS ONE 'BEFORE'."

"SEE? NOTHIN' WRONG WITH *MY* TEETH!"

"I CAME OVER TO PLAY WITH YA, MARGARET. I CAN'T FIND ANY BOYS."

"SURE PARENTS ARE A PAIN SOMETIMES, BUT YOU *GOTTA* HAVE 'EM.... UNLESS YOU GOT YOUR OWN HOUSE."

"I GOT A BIG RANCH IN TEXAS! WITH *SIXTEEN MILLION* COWS 'N HORSES! AN' TWO WHITE RATS."

"SEE? DIDN'T I TELL YA HE SLEEPS IN A *CRAZY* OUTFIT?"

"DENNIS, STOP WORRYING ABOUT ME! I'M *NATURALLY* THIN! AND I'LL *NEVER* BE HUSKY LIKE COWBOY BOB!"

"WELL, I'M SOLD!"

"WHY, NO, HE JUST *SPRAINED* HIS ARM! WHO TOLD YOU HE BROKE IT IN FOUR PLACES?"

"I GOT OUR HOSE, MR. WILSON! I'M GONNA
HELP YA!"

"THERE'S A GUY DOWNSTAIRS. BUT HE'S NOT A
BURGLAR 'CAUSE HE'S NOT WEARIN' A MASK."

"I **DID** GIVE HIM THE OL' ONE-TWO,
BUT HE CAN **COUNT** FASTER'N ME!"

"WOULD YOU PLEASE BLOW UP YOUR CHEST AGAIN? JOEY MISSED IT!"

"I WANT *EVERYTHING* ON MY HOTDOG! INCLUDIN' A *HAMBURGER!*"

"THIS ONE'S GOT A LOT OF GOOD READIN'
IN IT . . . . . IF YA LIKE PICTURES."

"WHATTA YA WANT ME TO DO? LET MY HANDS *DRIP* DRY?"

'YOU HEARD ME, SONNY! I'M NOT LEAVING UNTIL YOU CALL YOUR MOTHER . . . .'

"NOTICE HOW PEPPY RUFF IS ACTIN' SINCE
I BEEN GIVIN' HIM VITAMIN PILLS?"

"WANNA SEE A PRETTY WATERFALL?"

'I DON'T THINK HE'S FEELING WELL. *NOBODY'S* COMPLAINED ABOUT HIM ALL DAY!'

"AW, HE JUST GOT SCARED 'CAUSE I SAID I'D GIVE HIM A FREE HAIRCUT."

"HEY, MISTER WILSON! WHAT ARE THE LITTLE SIGNS FOR?"

"I JUST WANTED TO SEE IF I COULD REACH THE PEDALS!"

"IT'S JUST THE *BOTTOM* PART OF THE COOKIE JAR, MOM! LUCKY THING I LAID THE LID OVER THERE, HUH? HUH, MOM?"

"LUCKY WE CAME, DAD! LOOK--- *STEAK KNIVES!*"

"THIS IS A SONG ABOUT HOW MUCH COWBOY BOB'S HORSE LIKES HIM. IT'S CALLED SANDPAPER KISSES."

"BUT IF I DIDN'T INTERRUPT I'D NEVER GET TO SAY *ANYTHING!*"

"BOY, I HOPE ITS WORKIN' BY 'COWBOY BOB' TIME! YA THINK SO? HUH?
THAT'S NOT LONG, YA KNOW. THINK IT'LL BE WORKIN'? HUH? YA THINK
SO? . . ."

"DID YA KNOW IT WAS *ME* TALKIN'? HUH? DID YA SEE MY LIPS MOVE? HUH?..."

"WERE YOU BELLERIN' FOR ME?"

"*MOM!* MARGARET AN' GINA HAD A *FIGHT* OVER ME, AN' NOW THEY BOTH *HATE* ME!"

"HIS NAME IS BERT, BUT I CALL HIM MR. YACKETY YACK."

"I'll *NEVER* HAVE CHILDREN! DO YOU *HEAR* ME? *NEVER!*"

"ANYBODY SEEN A CAT? DAD SAYS THERE'S
A LOT OF *MEOWIN'* GOING ON IN HERE."

"OKAY IF I TAKE MY GRUB OUT UNDER THE STARS, MA'AM?"

"I FEEL SORRY FOR ANYBODY THAT STARTS SOMETHIN' WITH *THIS GUY!*"

"YA KNOW WHAT, MOM? JOEY SAYS HE *GOES* FOR BLONDS!"

"HEY, GINA! THIS MEANS *YOU!*"

"IT'S SORTA LIKE DUSTIN' WITH A CHICKEN, ISN'T IT?"

"I'M HERE 'CAUSE I'M NOT SLEEPY. *RUFF'S* HERE 'CAUSE YOU WHISTLE WHEN YOU SNORE."

"ANYBODY WANNA PLAY SOME THREE-HANDED BASKETBALL?"

"BUT, ALICE, I CAN'T RUN HOME EVERY TIME DENNIS DOES SOME LITTLE ...."

"...HE *WHAT*?"

"IT'S GONNA BE A LONG TIME BEFORE WE EAT.
YOU OUGHTA SEE ALL THE DIRTY DISHES!"

"THEY *OUGHTA* BE GOOD! ALL THE TELEBISION DOGS EAT 'EM!"

"THEY'RE CALLED FRECKLES, BUSTER. *FRECKLES*! NOT POLKA DOTS!"

"I SAID, *KEEP YOUR EYES OPEN!* I GOT FIVE
WHOLE DOLLARS IN YOUR BANK!"

I SEE WHAT YA MEAN, MOM. SHE *HAS* GOT A WHINY VOICE!°

"DID YA SEE *THAT*?! HE MADE HIS *OWN* CIGARETTE JUST LIKE A *REAL COWBOY*!"

"DON'T TAKE IT OFF! I TOL' JOEY YOU HAD A HAIRY CHEST!"

"I'LL GO TELL DENNIS YOU'RE JUST FIXING YOUR SPRINKLING SYSTEM. HE THOUGHT YOU WERE SETTING A BOOBY TRAP FOR HIM!"

"I'LL JUST PUT THESE ON . . . . . IN CASE
MY MOM LOOKS FOR FINGERPRINTS!"

"LISTEN, I *TOLD* YOU WE DIDN'T *HAVE* TERMITES! AND IF WE DID, YOU COULDN'T *HEAR* THEM!"

"MOTHER, I'M GOING TO BABY SIT FOR THE MITCHELLS. WOULD YOU LOAN ME ONE OF YOUR TRANQUILIZERS?"

"YOU'D LIKE MY DOG, _HE_ SLEEPS *ALL* THE TIME!"